WHAT'S INSIDE?
AIRCRAFT OF WORLD WAR II

WHAT'S INSIDE?
AIRCRAFT OF WORLD WAR II

Sandy Creek
NEW YORK

An Imprint of Sterling Publishing
387 Park Avenue South
New York, NY 10016

Editorial and design by
Amber Books Ltd
74–77 White Lion Street
London N1 9PF
United Kingdom

Series Editor: Michael Spilling
Design: Brian Rust and Andrew Easton
Picture Research: Terry Forshaw

ISBN 978-1-4351-5366-0

Manufactured in China
Lot #:
2 4 6 8 10 9 7 5 3 1
09/12

Picture Credits
Photographs
Art-Tech/Aerospace: 6–10 all, 12, 14, 16–20 all, 23–28 all, 31, 32, 35, 39, 40, 44
Art-Tech/MARS: 3, 30, 43
Cody Images: 22
Dreamstime: 11 (14Lcol2), 15 (Andrew Periam), 34 (Lee Ditch), 36 (Kenk), 38 (Martin Spurny)
U.S. Department of Defense: 42
Artworks
All artworks Amber Books/Peters & Zebransky

Contents

• • • • • • • • • • • • • • • • •

Junkers Ju 87B-2 Stuka

Early in World War II (1939–1945), Germany's Stuka dive-bombers swooped down to blast Allied positions from Poland to France. No other ground-attack warplane could match the Stuka's shock-effect.

The Stuka was built for "terror bombing." Sirens on each wing shrieked as it dived downward. Stukas were known for attacking troops and civilians fleeing war zones.

An Accurate Dive-Bomber

The single-engine Junkers Ju 87 Stuka **dive-bomber** was introduced in 1936. It had a two-man crew (pilot and rear gunner) and could dive accurately, firing machine guns and dropping bombs. The Stuka's top speed was 242 miles per hour (390 km/h) with a range of 311 miles (500 km). Armaments included three machine guns and

Stukas patrol over the Soviet Union during the winter. They are painted white, like snow, to camouflage them when parked on airfields on the ground.

one 551-pound (250 kg) bomb, as well as four 110-pound (50 kg) bombs, two underneath each wing.

Hitler's Terror Sirens

Some say Germany's leader, Adolf Hitler, wanted Stukas to have the terrifying sirens. Hitler believed in shocking the enemy. Stukas were, indeed, frightening, but they lacked speed, which made

A Stuka dive-bombs enemy targets in Poland in 1939. Stukas could dive straight down at a 90-degree angle and at 370 miles per hour (595 km/h).

them easy targets for Allied fighters. As Allied fighters increased in number, Stukas suffered heavy losses. So many were shot down that by 1945 only a few were still in service.

A total of 6,500 Stukas were built. They flew in conflicts from Spain to Russia, and anyone attacked by Stukas always remembered their wailing sirens.

Did you know?

• • • • • • • • • • • • • • • • •

• **Stuka pilots had to be very brave to dive at full speed then pull up at the last minute after dropping their bombs.**

• **Pilots might black out from the force of the dive, so Stukas had an automatic system that made the plane pull up by itself.**

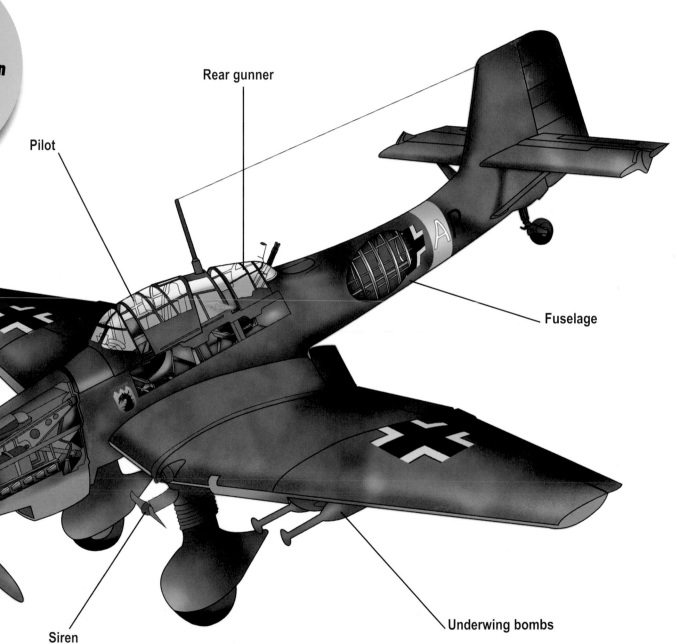

FACT
Stukas were first used in the Spanish Civil War (1936–1939), fighting for the Spanish fascists.

Rear gunner

Pilot

Fuselage

Siren

Underwing bombs

Avro Lancaster B. Mk I

Britain's Lancaster was the main strategic bomber of the Royal Air Force (RAF) in the war years 1942–1945. The "Lancs," as they were known, took part in 156,000 missions against German-occupied Europe.

Lancs mainly flew night bombing raids, carrying the largest Allied bomb, the 12,000-pound (5,400 kg) **blockbuster**. They became the most successful Allied night bomber of the war.

Strategic Bombing

The Lancaster was introduced in 1942, when the **Allies** began a **strategic bombing** offensive over Europe. The four-engine Lanc was the main **heavy bomber** in this campaign. The Lanc was used by the RAF as well as by Canadian and other **squadrons** from countries serving

A Lancaster with its landing gear down flies during an air show of World War II aircraft.

These Lancaster bombers are painted in the standard brown and green camouflage, which broke up their shape and dulled any shine.

designed to skip over the surface of the water and blow open the dams.

Late in the war, Lancasters dropped food into German-occupied Holland. The German forces there allowed this to happen so the people caught in the fighting would not starve.

with the Allies. It had a crew of seven, including a pilot, three gunners, and three specialists. It was 69 feet (21 m) long with a wingspan of 102 feet (31 m).

Bombs and Food

Lancasters also flew daylight missions, often carrying the 22,000-pound (10,000 kg) Grand Slam "earthquake" bomb. Lancs became more famous after the war as "Dam Busters," because of a popular movie about their wartime attack on important German dams. The Lancs flew dangerously low to drop the "bouncing bomb,"

Did you know?

• • • • • • • • • • • • • • • • • • • •

• To honor the Lancaster's war service, in 1946 one flew the first scheduled flight from the new London Heathrow Airport.

• Lancs also were used as flying tankers for refueling aircraft in flight. They even became high-speed passenger airliners and also carried mail across the Atlantic.

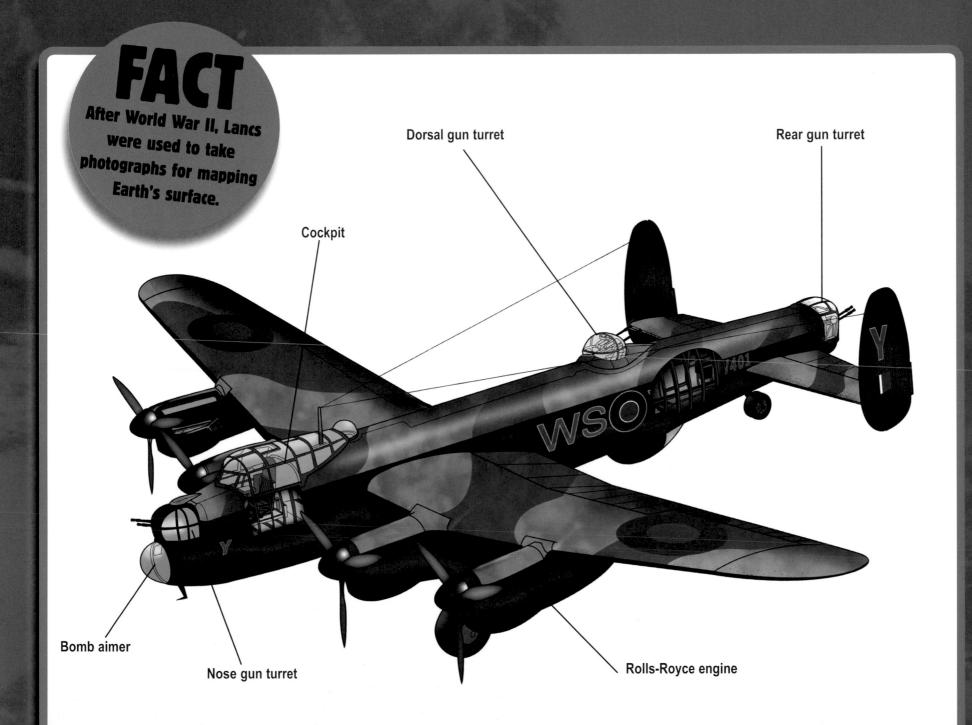

FACT
After World War II, Lancs were used to take photographs for mapping Earth's surface.

Dorsal gun turret

Rear gun turret

Cockpit

Bomb aimer

Nose gun turret

Rolls-Royce engine

Supermarine Spitfire Mk V

The single-engine Supermarine Spitfire was designed as a high-performance warplane for taking on enemy fighters. Britain's Spitfire fighter competed against Germany's Bf 109 to be the world's fastest aircraft.

During the air campaign called the Battle of Britain (July–October 1940), the Spitfire's success in **dogfights** made it one of the most famous aircraft of the war.

Handled Like a Sports Car

The Spitfire was joined by the Hawker Hurricane in the Royal Air Force's fighter defense of Britain. The Hurricane also was an excellent warplane. It was more maneuverable but not as fast as the Spitfire.

A restored Supermarine Spitfire touches down gracefully during an air show.

Did you know?

• **In the Battle of Britain, Spitfires attacked the fighters protecting the German bombers. Then the Hurricanes went after the bomber fleet.**

• **The machine guns that sat in the wings of the Spitfire also included heating—to stop the guns from freezing at high altitude.**

The Spitfire saw action wherever Allied troops campaigned. It was an interceptor, fighter-bomber, and **carrier-based fighter**. It also flew **photo reconnaissance**. The Spitfire had a sleek design. Pilots loved flying it. They said it was like driving a sports car.

Superior Spitfires

The builder of Spitfires was Supermarine Aviation Works, which improved the plane with each new model in its Mk (Mark) series: Mk I in 1940 to Mk XVIII (18) in 1945. The Mk V appeared in late 1940 and was superior to any aircraft of its day. The single-seat Spitfire had a wingspan of almost 37 feet (11.2 m) and a maximum speed of 378 mph (605 km/h). It had a combat range of 470 miles (760 km) and could reach a **ceiling** of 35,000 feet (11,300 m). More than 20,300 Spitfires were produced.

This wartime Mk XII (12) Spitfire flies through clouds as it banks to its left.

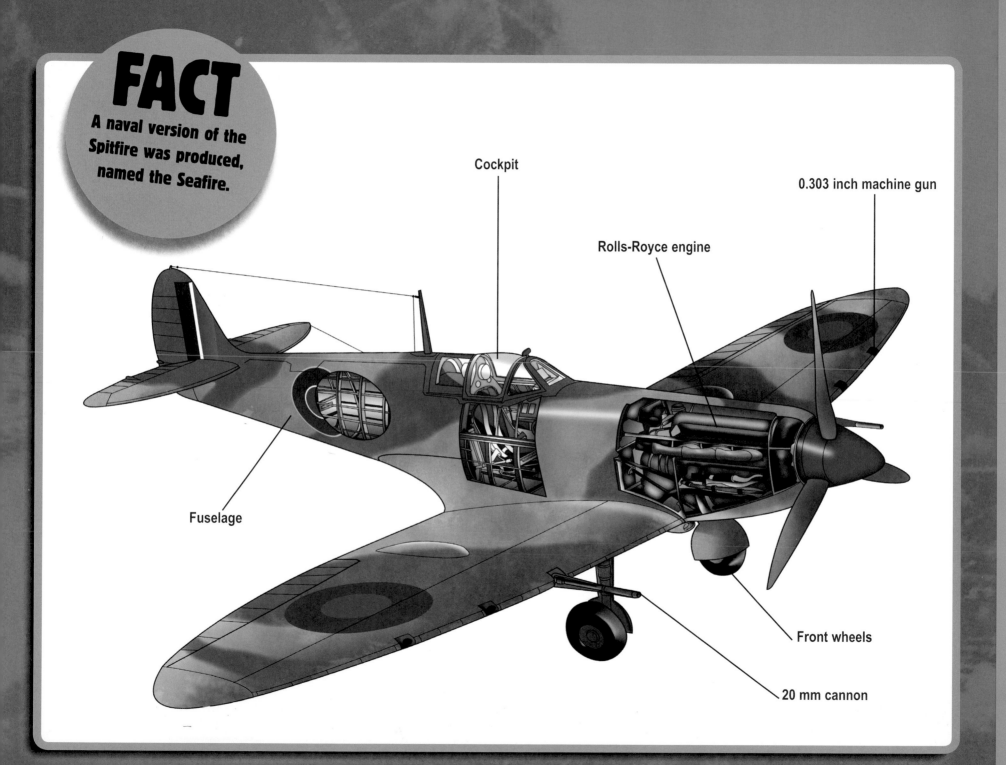

FACT

A naval version of the Spitfire was produced, named the Seafire.

Cockpit

Rolls-Royce engine

0.303 inch machine gun

Fuselage

Front wheels

20 mm cannon

Mitsubishi A6M Zero

At the start of World War II, Japan's Zero was one of the world's best fighter aircraft. In maneuvering and attacking, the speedy and light Zero could outfly the Allied fighters of the day.

Zeros flying from **aircraft carriers** made the December 1941 surprise attack on the American base at Pearl Harbor, Hawaii. The Zero became an essential weapon for Japan's navy.

Agile but Unarmored

The Zero was very fast but also **agile**. It could suddenly turn and open fire on surprised enemy pilots. By 1943, the Americans had a fighter to outdo the Zero: the Hellcat. Soon, A6M5-type Zeros were designed to take

A Japanese Zero demonstrates its speed and flying ability at a modern air show.

on the Hellcat. Zeros held their own, but they could not match the Hellcat in high-speed **maneuvers**. Also, Zeros had no armor to protect the pilot, and when hit by bullets, the fighter often caught fire.

When Japan was losing the war, the Zero became the main aircraft for **kamikaze** attacks. Pilots gave their lives flying head on to enemy warships to blow them up.

Did you know?

• **The name Zero was given by its pilots. This was because zero was the last digit of the Japanese year 2600 (1940), when the fighter entered service.**

• **At least 47 Allied vessels were sunk and 300 damaged by kamikaze attacks. Nearly 4,000 kamikaze pilots were killed.**

Specifications

The Zero had a wingspan of 39 feet (12 m) and flew at a maximum speed of 331 miles per hour (533 km/h). Its ceiling was 33,000 feet (10,000 m) and it had a range of 1,929 miles (3,105 km). Armament included machine guns, two 0.79 inch (20 mm) cannons, and two 132-pound (60 kg) bombs for kamikaze attacks.

Zeros parked at an airfield show Japan's air force disk marking on their wings and fuselage.

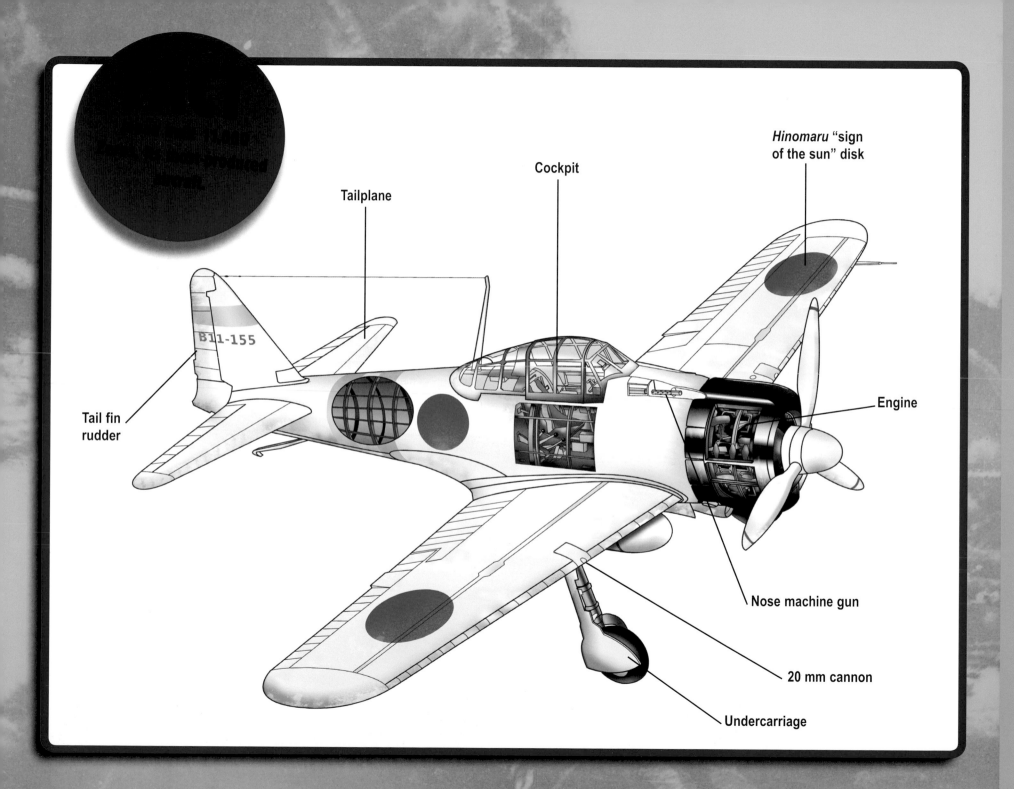

Tailplane

Cockpit

Hinomaru "sign of the sun" disk

B11-155

Tail fin rudder

Engine

Nose machine gun

20 mm cannon

Undercarriage

Messerschmitt Bf 109E

After its defeat in World War I (1914–1918), Germany prepared for the next war. It built an air force led by the Bf 109, the world's fastest fighter aircraft at the time.

The Bf 109 first went into action during the Spanish Civil War (1936–1939). The 109s were battle-tested by Germany against the enemies of the Spanish **fascists**.

Key to the Blitzkrieg

World War II began, and the 109 became the best-known aircraft in Germany's *Luftwaffe* (air force). In 1940, the 109 won **air superiority** for Germany during the *blitzkrieg* campaign that defeated France. The

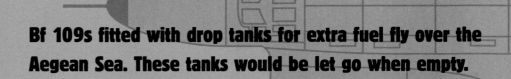

Bf 109s fitted with drop tanks for extra fuel fly over the Aegean Sea. These tanks would be let go when empty.

aircraft. The 109 served successfully in every German campaign until the end of the war in 1945.

The 109's wingspan was 32.5 feet (10 m), and its maximum speed reached 398 miles per hour (640 km/h), with a range of 528 miles (850 km). The 109 could climb to an **altitude** of 39,370 feet (12,000 m).

Allies knew this fighter as the Me 109. Me stood for Messerschmitt, the German aircraft manufacturer. To Allied servicemen who had to fight them, any Bf 109 was called a "Messerschmitt" or a "109." There were several types of Bf 109s (the 109K-4 was fastest of all).

Light and Quick

The single-seat, single-engine Bf 109 was light and built for speed. The 109 was an **interceptor**, but was developed to serve as a **bomber escort**, **ground-attack** fighter, **fighter-bomber**, and as a **reconnaissance**

Did you know?

• • • • • • • • • • • • • • • •

• **The three top German fighter aces of the war flew Bf 109s, with 928 victories between them. A total of 105 Bf 109 pilots each destroyed at least 100 Allied planes.**

• **The Bf 109 and Britain's Spitfire fighter competed to be the world's fastest aircraft.**

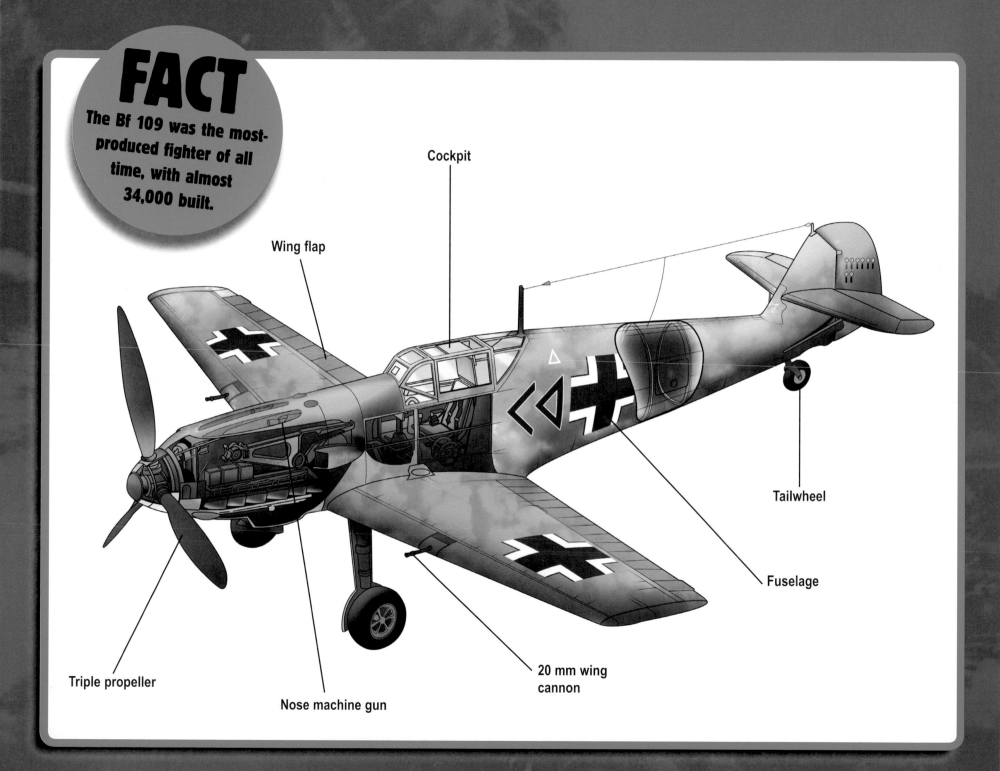

FACT

The Bf 109 was the most-produced fighter of all time, with almost 34,000 built.

Cockpit

Wing flap

Tailwheel

Fuselage

Triple propeller

Nose machine gun

20 mm wing cannon

Focke-Wulf Fw 190F-2

Germany's Focke-Wulf Fw 190 fighter plane fought with much success on many battlefronts. The Fw 190 was fast and maneuverable, used for air-to-air combat as well as for fighter-bomber and ground-attack duties.

● ● ● ● ● ● ● ● ● ● ● ● ● ● ● ● ●

Pilots liked the Fw 190 for its dependability in combat. They said the faster Bf 109 was a racehorse, but the Fw 190 was a tough cavalry horse.

Dependable, with Firepower

The single-seat, single-engine Fw 190 was introduced in mid-1941, in time for Germany's invasion of Russia. Many top pilots in the German air force preferred the Fw 190 for its flying ability at low altitudes. This ability was important when flying low on missions over England, when they had to fight off Spitfires. These pilots also

Early models of the Fw 190 are lined up at an airfield during testing in the summer of 1941.

favored the Fw 190's firepower over that of the Bf 109. The pilot could fire all his guns at once, or fire pairs of guns independently.

Quickly Back in Action

As the war went on, Fw 190s were improved in speed and firepower, but they remained strong and dependable. The Fw 190 could operate from rugged

Fw 190s fly over the Eastern Front, as the Soviet Union battle zone was termed.

frontline airfields and be easily maintained by mechanics. It took battle damage, was quickly repaired, and got back in the air.

The Fw 190's maximum speed was 426 miles per hour (685 km/h), and it had a ceiling of 39,370 feet (12,000 m). Its range was 519 miles (835 km). Its armaments included 0.79 inch (20 mm) cannons, bombs, rockets, and sometimes anti-ship **torpedoes**.

Did you know?

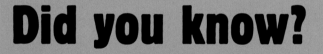

• **Against the Soviets, the Fw 190 was especially effective at attacking supply columns, destroying trucks and even tanks.**

• **More than 20,000 Fw 190s were built. During top production, 22 were turned out every day. At the war's end, about 1,600 remained.**

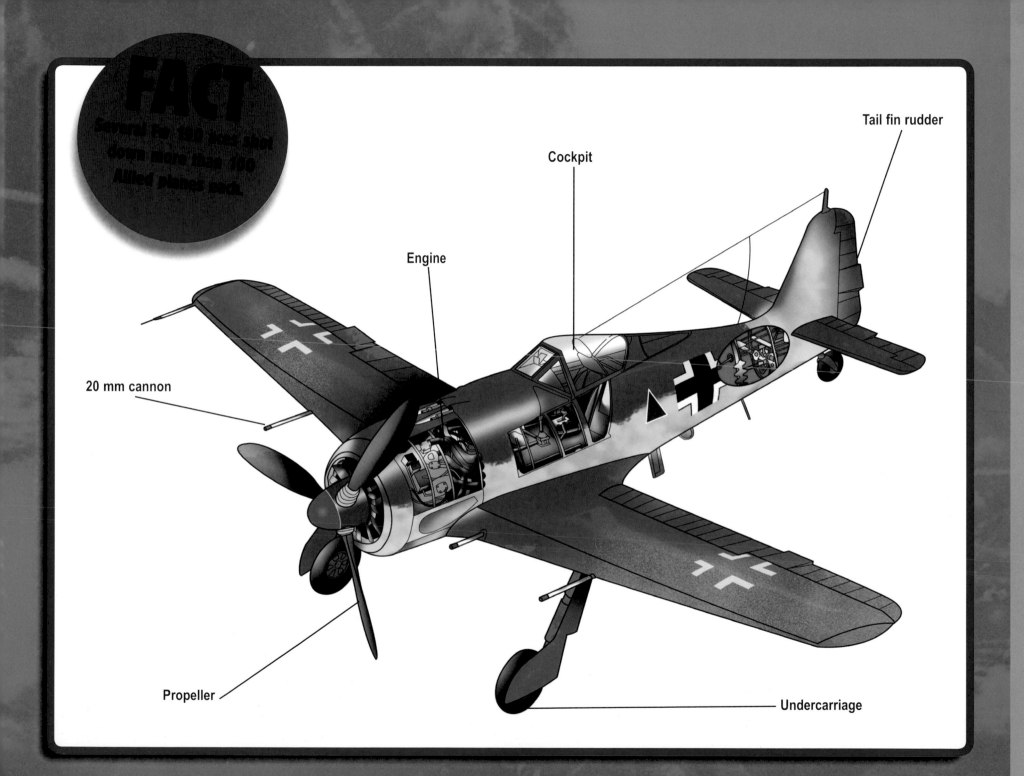

FACT

Several Fw 190 Aces shot down more than 100 Allied planes each.

Tail fin rudder

Cockpit

Engine

20 mm cannon

Propeller

Undercarriage

Grumman F6F Hellcat

On December 7, 1941, Japanese warplanes attacked the U.S. Navy base at Pearl Harbor, Hawaii. The United States entered World War II against Japan and other Axis powers, and American aircraft carriers went into action.

To win the war at sea, the U.S. Navy needed a carrier fighter to match Japan's Mitsubishi Zero. The Grumman Hellcat was designed to meet that challenge.

Hellcat against Zero

The Grumman Aircraft company worked through 1942 and 1943 to develop the Hellcat. In September 1943, Hellcats first took on a force of Zeros and shot down 30 of them. Only one Hellcat was lost. Hellcats were faster **climbers** and their pilots more experienced in combat

This early F6F-3 Hellcat model had extra cockpit armor and a bullet-resistant windshield. It could carry bombs or ground attack rockets.

than Japan's. For the next two years, the United States led Allied forces in the war in the Pacific. Month after month, the Allies steadily advanced toward Japan.

A Decisive Victory

In the June 1944 Battle of the Philippine Sea, the U.S. Navy won the war's last great carrier-against-carrier

action. Hellcats led the combat, which cost Japan more than 650 warplanes. The Americans lost 123 planes. The Hellcat was a rugged aircraft, with a speed of 380 miles per hour (621 km/h) and a **combat range** of 945 miles (1,520 km). Its ceiling was 37,300 feet (11,370 m). The Hellcat's armaments included machine guns, rockets, bombs, and torpedoes.

American airmen were nicknamed "fly boys." These two open their Hellcat cockpits for a photograph over the Pacific.

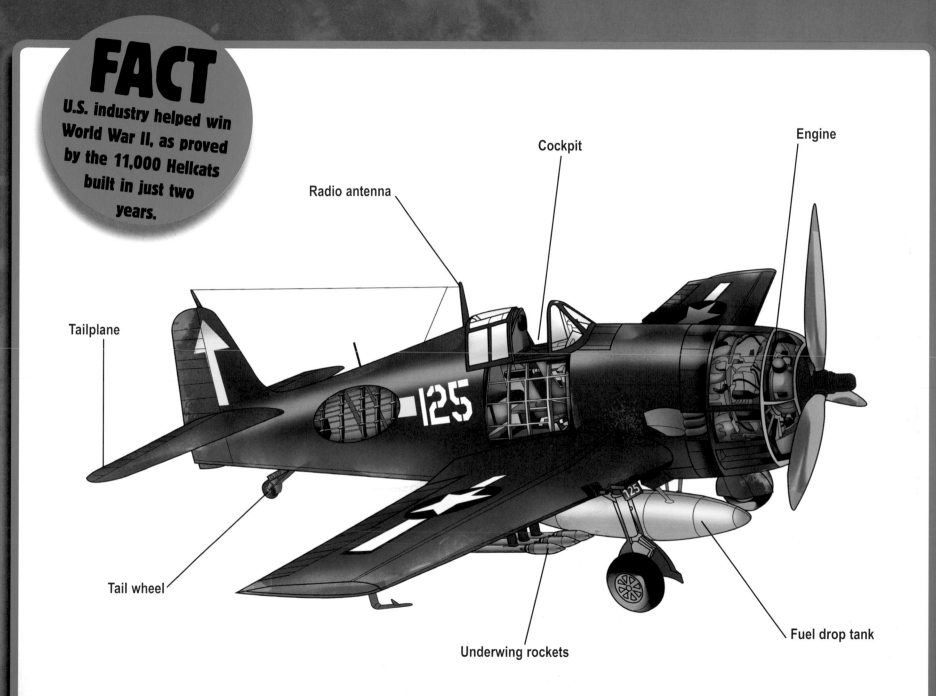

FACT

U.S. industry helped win World War II, as proved by the 11,000 Hellcats built in just two years.

Cockpit

Engine

Radio antenna

Tailplane

Tail wheel

Underwing rockets

Fuel drop tank

125

North American P-51D Mustang

The P-51 Mustang was the best U.S. escort fighter and dogfighter. Faster than the German Bf 109s and Fw 190s, the P-51 also handled better at high altitude, where it protected Allied bombers.

In 1943, the P-51D became the first Allied fighter with a range long enough to escort heavy bombers on missions from Britain to strike targets in Germany.

Long-Range Fighter

The Allies had short-range fighters that could go against the German Bf 109s and Fw 190s in the battle for air superiority over Britain. Many considered the Spitfire a better fighter than the P-51. The P-51, however, could

U.S. P-51 Mustang fighters of the 375th Fighter Squadron fly in formation on a mission over Europe in 1944.

P-51 Mustangs remain a popular attraction at air shows. After World War II, many were sold for personal use or for air racing.

(700 km/h) and a range of 1,650 miles (1,430 km). Its ceiling was 41,900 feet (12,800 m). The P-51 was armed with six machine guns, its main weapons for aerial combat. It could also carry bombs and rockets for attacking ground targets.

hold enough fuel to fly much farther. P-51 fighters escorted U.S. bombers to targets as far away as Berlin, the German capital. With the P-51 to protect them, Allied bombers could strike at any time, night or day.

Top U.S. Fighter in Europe

The P-51 became the main American fighter in Europe. Few P-51s served in the Pacific, where the carrier-based Grumman Hellcat was the most important U.S. fighter. The P-51 had a maximum speed of 437 miles per hour

Did you know?

• The Tuskegee Airmen, a famous African-American fighter unit, became known for their great success flying P-51 Mustangs on bomber escort missions.

• The P-51 was such an effective fighter that it stayed in service in some air forces until the 1980s.

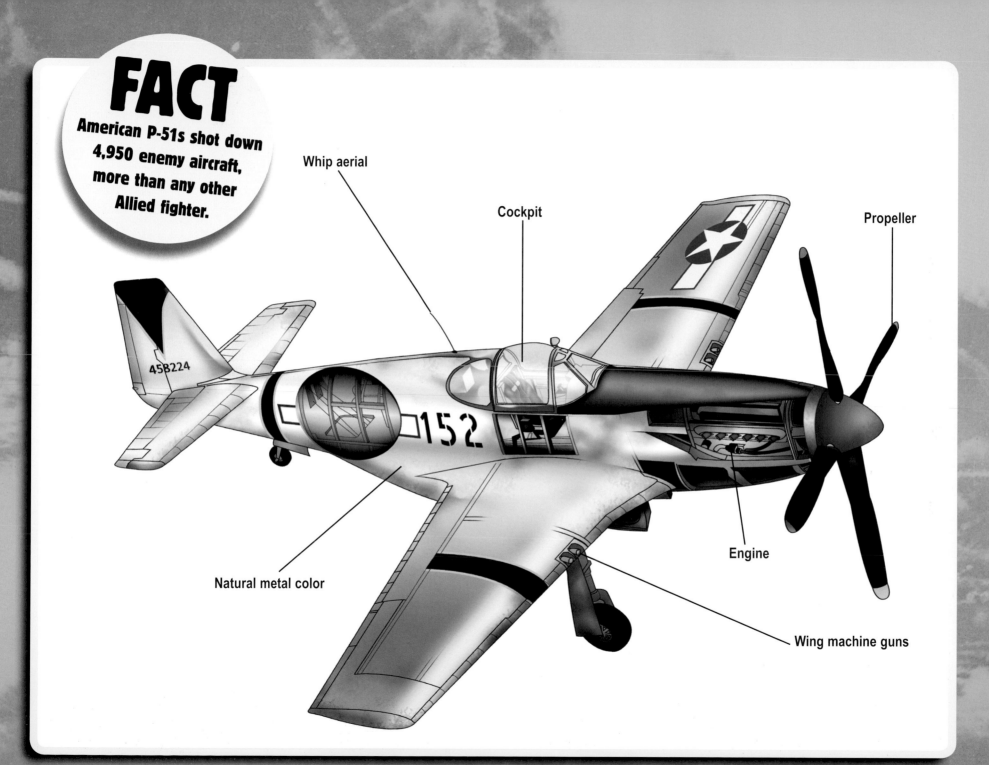

FACT

American P-51s shot down 4,950 enemy aircraft, more than any other Allied fighter.

Whip aerial

Cockpit

Propeller

458224

152

Natural metal color

Engine

Wing machine guns

Yakovlev Yak-3

The Yakovlev Yak-3 was an air superiority fighter introduced by the Soviet Union in 1944. Soon after Yak-3s entered the war on the Eastern Front, the Red Army won control of the skies.

The Yak-3 was small and light with a powerful engine. This made it one of the fastest, most agile fighters of the war.

Feared Yak-3 Fighter

The Soviet Union needed a fighter to counter Germany's high-performing Bf 109s. The Yak-3 came late to the war and served from 1944 to 1945. It had a short combat range, but soon won many victories. German fighter pilots were even ordered to avoid combat with Yak-3s. Soviet pilots and ground crews liked its

A Yak-3 with the Soviet red star on its fuselage. Yak-3s helped the Soviets defeat the German _Luftwaffe_.

tough design. The Yak-3 was easy to repair and could be built cheaply.

Small, Light, and Quick

Some thought the Yak-3 was a better dogfighter than even the Spitfire or P-51 Mustang. It was the lightest of the top

France's Normandy-Neimen fighter squadron flying Yak-3s fought alongside the Soviets from 1943 to 1945.

World War II fighters and could outmaneuver most planes. The Yak-3 had a maximum speed of 407 miles per hour (655 km/h) and a range of 405 miles (650 km). Its ceiling was 35,000 feet (10,700 m). The Yak-3 was armed with two machine guns and a cannon. Built mainly for aerial combat, it did not carry bombs. More than 4,800 were produced.

Did you know?

• The Yak-3 was the smallest fighter in World War II, with a length of 27 feet 10 inches (98.5 m) and a wingspan of 30 feet 2 inches (9.2 m).

• The Yak-3's guns were built into its nose and not in the wings. This made the wings lighter, making the fighter more maneuverable.

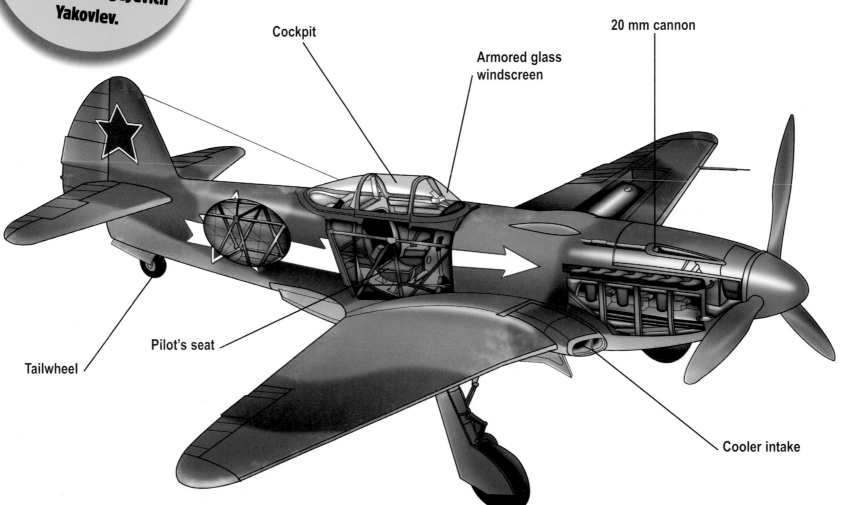

Cockpit

Armored glass windscreen

20 mm cannon

Pilot's seat

Tailwheel

Cooler intake

Boeing B-29 Superfortress

The U.S. B-29 Superfortress carried out fire bombing missions against Japan during World War II. The most famous B-29 mission was the dropping of atomic bombs on Japan to end the war.

• • • • • • • • • • • • • • • • •

The B-29 was a strategic bomber, meaning it flew at high altitudes. B-29s reached 31,850 feet (9,710 m), above the Japanese fighters and the range of antiaircraft guns.

Fire Bombing

When high-altitude bombing was not effective enough, B-29s were used in low-altitude night missions. Then they dropped **napalm** bombs to set cities ablaze. At 99 feet (30 m) long with a wingspan of 141 feet (43 m), the B-29 was one of the largest aircraft of the war. The four-engine B-29 could carry 20,000 pounds (9,100 kg) of bombs to

The B-29 named "Eddie Allen" sits on a runway during one of its first missions. It is named after a test pilot killed in a crash of an early B-29.

manning the **radar** and radio. Superforts were mainly flown by U.S. forces. The B-29 Enola Gay is the most famous aircraft of the war. In August 1945, Enola Gay dropped the atomic bomb on Hiroshima, beginning the era of atomic power.

From 1943 to 1946, 3,970 Superforts were built. Their last combat missions were during the Korean War (1950–1953).

The B-29 was the first super heavy bomber flown by any air force. It could hit targets at great distances with large bombs.

targets more than 2,660 miles (4,290 km) distant. Its top speed was 357 miles per hour (574 km/h).

Superfort

Nicknamed "Superfort," the B-29 had a crew of 11, including a pilot and copilot, three gunners, and six others whose duties ranged from aiming bombs to

Did you know?

• One of the most dangerous duties in all of World War II was the tail gunner in bombers such as the B-29. He had to fight off enemy warplanes attacking from behind—and usually aiming right at him.

• A Superfort carried up to 12,000 rounds of ammunition, so its gunners could fire nonstop at enemy fighters.

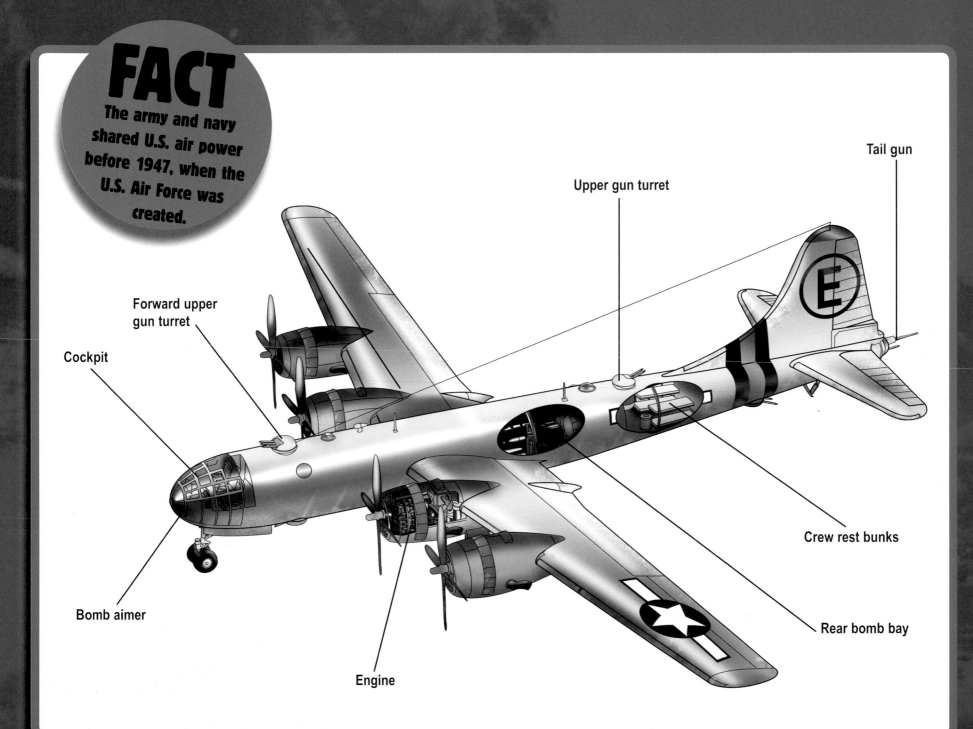

FACT
The army and navy shared U.S. air power before 1947, when the U.S. Air Force was created.

Upper gun turret

Tail gun

Forward upper gun turret

Cockpit

Crew rest bunks

Bomb aimer

Rear bomb bay

Engine

Glossary

ace—a pilot who has shot down at least five enemy aircraft

agile—the ability to move easily and quickly

air superiority—having control of air combat

aircraft carrier—a warship that is a base for aircraft

Allies (The)—nations against Germany and her supporting nations in World Wars I and II

altitude—height above the ground

Axis (The)—Germany, Japan, Italy, and supporting countries in World War II

bank—when an aircraft tilts to the side while making a turn

blitzkrieg—a conflict fought with great speed and force

blockbuster—a large, powerful bomb dropped from the air

bomber escort—fighters that protect bombers

camouflage—disguise for military equipment

carrier-based fighter—fighters that use aircraft carriers

ceiling—an aircraft's highest altitude

climber—aircraft that can fly up quickly

cockpit—the space in an aircraft for the pilot and flight crew

combat range—the maximum distance an aircraft can safely fly then return to base

dive-bomber—a warplane designed to dive and drop bombs

dogfights—air-to-air combat between fighter planes

drop tanks—extra fuel tanks

fascist—a state with few individual freedoms

fighter-bomber—an aircraft for aerial combat and bombing missions

fuselage—body of an aircraft

ground-attack warplane—aircraft that attacks targets on the ground

heavy bomber—long-range aircraft carrying large numbers of bombs

interceptor—fighter plane built to stop hostile aircraft

kamikaze—Japanese aircraft that crashed into Allied targets to blow them up

maneuver—controlled movement of an aircraft

napalm—a highly flammable substance

photo reconnaissance—taking aerial photos of the enemy

radar—a system using radio waves to detect hostile planes

reconnaissance—gathering information in hostile territory

squadron—an air force unit

strategic bombing—the bombing of industrial targets that damages a country's ability to wage war

tail gunner—gunner at the rear of the plane

torpedo—a self-propelled missile that travels underwater

Index